The Step-by-St
Way to Draw Tiger

A Fun and Easy Drawing Book to Learn How to Draw
Tigers

By

Kristen Diaz.

License Notes

No part of this Book can be reproduced in any form or by any means including print, electronic, scanning or photocopying unless prior permission is granted by the author.

All ideas, suggestions and guidelines mentioned here are written for informative purposes. While the author has taken every possible step to ensure accuracy, all readers are advised to follow information at their own risk. The author cannot be held responsible for personal and/or commercial damages in case of misinterpreting and misunderstanding any part of this Book

Table of Contents

Introduction 4

How to draw a roaring tiger! 5

How to draw a sitting tiger! 21

How to draw a stalking tiger! 37

About the Author 53

Introduction

Becoming a great artist requires creativity, patience and practice. These habits can flourish in children when they start to develop them at a young age. We believe our guide will teach your child the discipline and patience required to not just learn to draw well, but to use those qualities in everything they do. Your job as a parent is to work with your child and encourage them when stuck and feel like giving up.

The world of art is an amazing way for you and your child to communicate and bond. When you open this book and start to create with your little one, you will delight in the things you learn about them and they will feel closer to you. Your support and gentle suggestions will help them be more patient with themselves and soon they will take the time needed to create spectacular drawings of which you can both be proud.

This guide is useful for parents as it teaches fundamentals of drawing and simple techniques. By following this book with your child, adults will learn patience and develop their skills as a child's most important teacher. By spending a few hours together you will develop a strong connection and learn the best ways of communicating with each other. It is truly a rewarding experience when you and your child create a masterpiece by working together!

How to draw a roaring tiger!

Step 1.

Let's design a series of cute tiger cubs having fun! Start by drawing a circle for the head and add some ears on top. Add a small nose and an indication of where the snout will be. Then the outline of the body.

Step 2.

Add the outline of the front legs and paws to the body.

Step 3.

Now draw her hind legs extended, as if she's making a fierce

stance.

Step 4.

Add a big smooth shape behind the body for the tail.

Step 5.

Our tiger cub is looking upwards, with its snout blocking the right side of its head. Draw an oval shape which surrounds the eye. Then add a curved line for the eye, which is closed. Then redraw the snout to smooth it out and from the W shapes upper jaw. Draw two sharp fangs and a row of teeth to the upper jaw. Her lower jaw is hanging open, so we can see the teeth of the bottom jaw as well. Finish is with a tongue and the inside of the mouth.

Step 6.

Tigers have a good amount of fur! Draw lots of spikes of fur around the cheeks, the ears and the top of the head. The cheeks are a different color than the rest of the body, so separate it by drawing soft plucks of fur in either directions.

Step 7.

Draw the fur on the chest of the tiger. Make it full to make it seem fluffy. Then redraw the paws and toes to make them smoother.

Step 8.

Now reshape the hind legs to complete their fierce stance. Add

the toes to the feet to finish them!

Step 9.

Add a line to separate the belly from the body and add the curved line to make the tip of the tail.

Step 10.

Tigers have cool stripes all over their body. Use the example to help you out or create your own awesome stripes!

Step 11.

Done! How does yours look? Let's color!

Step 12.

Tigers are known for their orange colored fur. While the majority is orange, it also has a white snout, belly, feet and toes. Some even have a white color for the tip of their tail! Don't forget to add white to the shape around the eye!

Step 13.

Give her it shadow and highlights to make her come to life!

Step 14.

Colored version. Look! She's roaring on the top of a cliff!

Step 15.

Line art version.

How to draw a sitting tiger!

Step 1.

The next tiger cub is going to be sitting. Start by drawing a circle for the head and add some ears on top. Add a small nose and an indication of where the snout will be. Then the outline of the body.

Step 2.

Add the outline of the front legs and paws to the body.

Step 3.

Now draw her hind legs. Add two ovals for the upper leg and two
rectangles for the paws..

Step 4.

Add a big smooth shape behind the body for the tail.

Step 5.

Our tiger cub is looking straight at us. Draw an oval shape which surrounds the eye. Then add another oval to each shape for the eye. Add a small eyelash to the side of the eye.   Now, redraw the snout to smooth it out and from the W shapes upper jaw. Draw two sharp in each corner and have her tongue sticking out, as if she's challenging us.

Step 6.

Tigers have a good amount of fur around the head! Draw lots of spikes of fur around the cheeks, the ears and the top of the head. The cheeks are a different color than the rest of the body, so separate it by drawing soft plucks of fur in either directions.

Step 7.

Draw the fur on the chest, but not a lot, as this is a very young

cub. Then redraw the paws and toes to complete them.

Step 8.

Now we go to the hind legs. We won't need to do much as the oval shapes for the leg is in the correct position. Simply redraw the paws and add the toes.

Step 9.

Add a line to separate the belly from the body, and close the top of the chest. Lastly, add the curved line to make the tip of the tail.

Step 10.

Tigers have cool stripes all over their body which are usually mirrored on either side of it. Use the example to help you out or create your own awesome stripes!

Step 11.

Done! How does yours look? Let's color!

Step 12.

Tigers are known for their orange colored fur. While the majority is orange, it also has a white snout, belly, feet and toes. Don't forget to add white to the shape around the eye! While some have white tips, we color the tip of this tail black.

Step 13.

Give her it shadow and highlights to make her come to life!

Step 14.

Colored version. Look! She's sitting on a giant mushroom!

Step 15.

Line art version.

How to draw a stalking tiger!

Step 1.

The next tiger cub is going to be stalking; a fancy word to describe a tiger nearing her prey. Start by drawing a circle for the head and add some ears on top. Add a small nose and an indication of where the snout will be. Then the outline of the body.

Step 2.

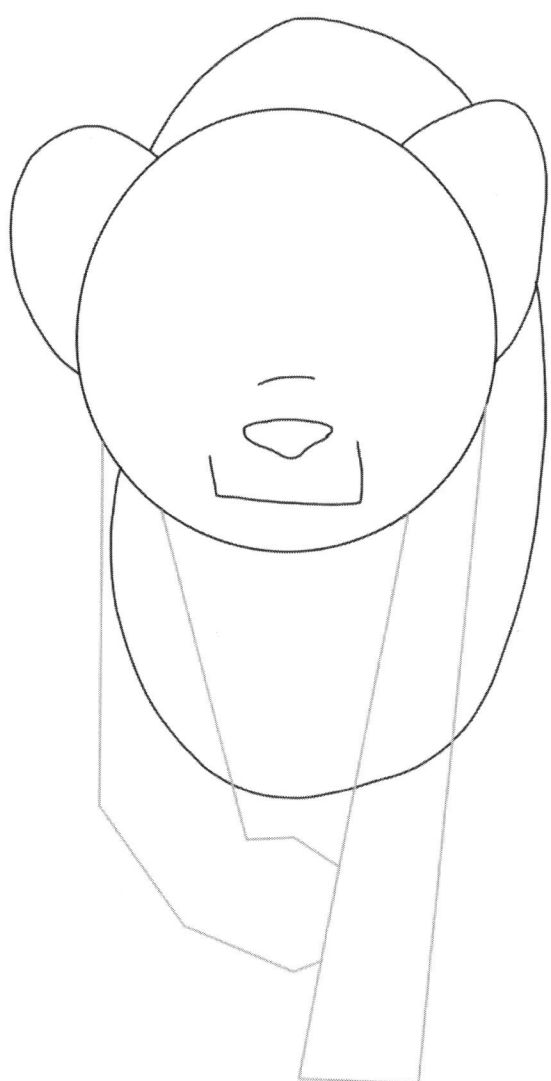

Add the outline of the front legs and paws to the body. Have the right leg curled up to show that she's walking.

Step 3.

The hind legs are mostly hidden behind the body. We can barely make out the feet.

Step 4.

Add a big smooth shape behind the body for the tail. Most of it is hidden behind the body, so we can only see parts of it.

Step 5.

Our tiger cub is looking straight at us. Draw an oval shape which surrounds the eye. Then add another oval to each shape for the eye. Add a small eyelash to the side of the eye. Now, redraw the snout to smooth it out and from the W shapes upper jaw. Draw two sharp in each corner and have her mouth slightly open, as if she's ready to charge.

Step 6.

Tigers have a good amount of fur around the head! Draw lots of spikes of fur around the cheeks, the ears and the top of the head. The cheeks are a different color than the rest of the body, so separate it by drawing soft plucks of fur in either directions.

Step 7.

Draw the fur on the chest. Add a good amount to it, to show that she's old enough to hunt. Then redraw the paws and toes to complete them. Remember the paw pointing inwards to show that she's walking.

Step 8.

Now we go to the hind legs. As we don't see them very well, only draw the toes sticking out.

Step 9.

Now add the curved line to make the tip of the tail.

Step 10.

Tigers have cool stripes all over their body which are usually mirrored on either side of it. Use the example to help you out or create your own awesome stripes!

Step 11.

Done! How does yours look? Color time!

Step 12.

Tigers are known for their orange colored fur. While the majority is orange, it also has a white snout, belly, feet and toes. Her eyes are blue, to offset the warm orange colors. Don't forget to add white to the shape around the eye! While some have white tips, we color the tip of this tail black.

Step 13.

Give her it shadow and highlights to make her come to life!

Step 14.

Colored version. Look! She's sitting on a giant mushroom!

Step 15.

Line art version.

About the Author

Kristen Diaz is an accomplished artist and e-book author living in Southern California. She has provided the illustrations for hundreds of children's books as her realistic and lifelike images appeal to children and adults alike.

Diaz began her career as an artist when she was in her 20's creating caricatures on the beaches of sunny California. What started as a way to make extra spending money turned into a successful career because of her amazing talent. Her comically accurate caricatures had a unique look and one of the local authors took notice. When the writer asked Diaz to illustrate one of her books, Kristen jumped at the opportunity to showcase her talent. The result was spectacular and soon Diaz was in high demand. Her ability to change her style to fit the books made her an attractive artist to work with.

She decided to get a more formal education in graphic design and illustration by enrolling in the Arts program at Platt's College which is where she met the love of her life and life partner, Terri. The two live in Pasadena close to the beach where Diaz' career first flourished. She occasionally hangs out on the beach with her easel and paints and makes caricatures of the humanity passing by. Her e-books are simple to follow and contain many witty anecdotes about her life in Pasadena.

Printed in Great Britain
by Amazon